رَبّ

My Lord
Qur'anic Prayers for Daily Blessings & Inspiration

Mourad Diouri

مراد الديوري

My Lord: Qur'anic Prayers for Daily Blessings & Inspiration

First published in 2023
By Mosaic Tree Press

ISBN 978-1-916524-51-4

Book Design & Typesetting: Mosaic Tree Press

Browse our complete catalogue of publications at MosaicTree.org

Published by
Mosaic Tree Press

بسم الله الرحمن الرحيم

In the name of God, the Most Gracious, the Most Merciful

رَبّ

Rabbi

الْحَمْدُ لِلَّهِ رَبِّ الْعَالَمِينَ

الْحَمْدُ لِلَّهِ رَبِّ الْعَالَمِينَ

Alḥamdu lillāhi rabbil ʿālamīn

All praise is for Allah, Lord of all worlds.

[Al-Fatiḥah 1:2]

When should you say this prayer?

When expressing gratitude to Allah, acknowledging His lordship over all creation, and praising Him for His blessings and mercy on the entire universe.

رَبّ

Rabbi

رَبِّ زِدْنِي عِلْمًا

رَبِّ زِدْنِي عِلْمًا

Rabbi ziдnī ʿilman

O Lord, increase me in knowledge.

[Taha 20:114]

When should you say this prayer?

When pursuing knowledge and wisdom, asking for divine guidance in academic or spiritual endeavours, seeking better understanding and enlightenment.

رَبّ

Rabbi

رَبّ اشْرَحْ لِي صَدْرِي

رَبِّ اشْرَحْ لِي صَدْرِي

وَ يَسِّرْ لِي أَمْرِي

وَ يَسِّرْ لِي أَمْرِي

Rabbi Shraḥ lī ṣadrī

O Lord, lift up my heart.

[Taha 20:25]

When should you say this prayer?

When facing challenges or difficulties, asking for divine assistance and seeking emotional strength, clarity, and ease in dealing with life's trials.

Wa yassir lī ʾamrī

And make my task easy.

[Taha 20:26]

When should you say this prayer?

When faced with a decision or task, seeking divine help and ease in managing affairs, requesting smooth and favourable outcomes in personal or professional matters.

رَبِّ

Rabbi

رَبِّ إِنِّي ظَلَمْتُ نَفْسِي فَاغْفِرْ لِي

رَبِّ إِنِّي ظَلَمْتُ نَفْسِي فَاغْفِرْ لِي

Rabbi 'innī zalamtu nafsī fa ghfir lī

My Lord! I have definitely wronged my soul, so forgive me.

[Al-Qasas 28:16]

When should you say this prayer?

When seeking forgiveness from Allah for personal wrongs and sins, recognising one's shortcomings and seeking divine mercy and forgiveness.

رَبّ

Rabbi

رَبِّ ارْحَمْهُمَا

كَمَا رَبَّيَانِي صَغِيرًا

رَّبِّ ارْحَمْهُمَا كَمَا رَبَّيَانِي صَغِيرًا

Rabbi irḥamhuma kamā rabbayānī ṣaghīra

O Lord, have mercy on them (my parents), just as they cared for me when I was little.

[Al-isrā' 17:24]

When should you say this prayer?

When requesting mercy for one's parents, recognising their vital role in our upbringing, and seeking Allah's compassion for them as they once showed mercy to to us during our childhood.

رَبّ

Rabbi

رَبِّ هَبْ لِي مِنَ الصَّالِحِينَ

رَبِّ هَبْ لِي مِنْ الصَّالِحِينَ

Rabbi hab lī minaṣ-ṣāliḥīn

Lord, grant me a righteous son.

[Aṣ-Ṣāfāt 37:100]

When should you say this prayer?

When desiring virtuous companionship, asking for righteous individuals and companions in life, and seeking the company of those who lead to goodness and moral excellence.

رَبّ

Rabbi

إِنّي أَخَافُ اللَّه رَبَّ الْعَالَمِينَ

إِنِّي أَخَافُ الله رَبَّ الْعَالَمِينَ

'Innī akhāfu-llāha rabbal 'ālamīn

I truly fear Allah, the Lord of all worlds.

[Al-Hashr 59:16]

When should you say this prayer?

When recognising the fear of Allah, expressing awe and humility before the Lord of the worlds, and seeking protection and guidance in devout awareness.

رَبّ

Rabbi

أَعوذُ بِرَبِّ الْفَلَقِ

أَعُوذُ بِرَبِّ الْفَلَقِ

أَعوذُ بِرَبِّ النَّاسِ

أَعُوذُ بِرَبِّ النَّاسِ

A' ūdhu birabbin-nās

I seek refuge in the Lord of humankind.

[An-naas 114:1]

When should you say this prayer?

When seeking refuge in the Lord of the Dawn, asking for protection from harmful forces, and invoking divine shelter against the evils that may arise with the onset of daybreak.

A' ūdhu birabbil-falaq

I seek refuge in the Lord of the daybreak

[Al-Falaq 113:1]

When should you say this prayer?

When seeking refuge in the Lord of mankind, asking for protection from the harm that may come from fellow human beings, and invoking divine safeguarding against negative influences.

رَبّ

Rabbi

رَبِّ انْصُرْنِي بِمَا كَذَّبُونِ

رَبِّ انْصُرْنِي بِمَا كَذَّبُونِ

Rabbi nṣurnī bimā kaдh-дhaabūnī

Noah prayed, "My Lord! Help me, because they have denied me."

[Al-Mu'minun 23:26]

When should you say this prayer?

When facing opposition or false accusations, seeking Allah's support and assistance in the face of challenges, and asking for victory over those who deny the truth.

رَبِّ

Rabbi

رَبِّ انصُرْنِي عَلَى الْقَوْمِ الْمُفْسِدِينَ

رَبِّ انصُرْنِي عَلَى الْقَوْمِ الْمُفْسِدِينَ

Rabbi nṣurnī ʿalāl qawmil-mufsidīna

My Lord! Help me against the people of corruption.

[Al-'Ankabut 29:30]

When should you say this prayer?

When confronting a group of mischief-makers or wrongdoers, seeking divine aid and support against those who spread corruption and injustice.

رَبِّ

Rabbi

رَبِّ فَلَا تَجْعَلْنِي فِي الْقَوْمِ الظَّالِمِينَ

رَبِّ فَلَا تَجْعَلْنِي فِي الْقَوْمِ الظَّالِمِينَ

Rabbi falā tajʿalnī fīl-qawmidh-dhālimīna

My Lord, do not count me among the wrongdoing people.

[Al-Mu'minun 23:94]

When should you say this prayer?

When fearing inclusion among oppressors or wrongdoers, seeking Allah's protection from becoming part of an unjust community, and desiring to be on the side of justice.

رَبّ

Rabbi

◆

رَبِّ اجْعَلْ لِي آيَةً

رَبِّ اجْعَلْ لِي آيَةً

Rabbi j'al lī ayah

My Lord! Grant me a sign.

[Maryam 19:10]

When should you say this prayer?

When making a supplication for a
sign or miracle from Allah, expressing
a desire for a divine manifestation to
strengthen faith or serve as evidence.

رَبّ

Rabbi

رَبّ أَرِني أَنْظُرْ إِلَيْكَ

رَبّ أَرِني أَنْظُرْ إِلَيْكَ

Rabbi 'arini anzur 'ilayka

When Moses came at the appointed time and his Lord spoke to him, he asked, "My Lord! Reveal Yourself to me so I may see You."

[Al-A'raf 7:143]

When should you say this prayer?

When longing for a glimpse of Allah's presence, seeking a spiritual connection, and expressing a deep desire to behold the divine.

رَبّ

Rabbi

رَبّ اغْفِرْ وَارْحَمْ وَأَنْتَ خَيْرُ الرَّاحِمِينَ

رَبّ اغْفِرْ وَارْحَمْ وَأَنْتَ خَيْرُ الرَّاحِمِينَ

*Rabbi ghfir wa-rḥam wa 'anta khayrur-
rāḥimīna*

My Lord! Forgive and have mercy, for You are the best of those who show mercy.

[Al-Mu'minun 23:118]

When should you say this prayer?

When seeking forgiveness and mercy
from Allah, acknowledging His
superior compassion, and recognising
His infinite kindness.

رَبّ

Rabbi

رَبِّ أَنزِلْنِي مُنزَلًا مُبَارَكًا وَأَنتَ خَيْرُ الْمُنزِلِينَ

رَبِّ أَنزِلْنِي مُنْزَلًا مُبَارَكًا وَأَنْتَ خَيْرُ الْمُنزِلِينَ

Rabbi ʿanzilnī munzalan mubārakan wa ʾanta khayrul munzilīna

My Lord, let me land with Your blessing: it is You who provide the best landings.

[Al-Mu'minun 23:29]

When should you say this prayer?

When praying for a blessed place of residence or a positive life change, and recognising Allah as the best provider and bestower of blessings.

رَبّ

Rabbi

رَبّ إِنِّي لِمَا أَنزَلْتَ إِلَيَّ مِنْ خَيْرٍ فَقِيرٌ

رَبّ إِنِّي لِمَا أَنزَلْتَ إِلَيَّ مِنْ خَيْرٍ فَقِيرٌ

Rabbi 'innī limā 'anzalta 'ilayya min khayrin faqīr

My Lord! I am truly in (desperate) need of whatever provision You may have in store for me.

[Al-Qasas 28:24]

When should you say this prayer?

When acknowledging our dependence on Allah's goodness, expressing neediness, and seeking sustenance from His divine abundance.

رَبّ

Rabbi

رَبّ ابْنِ لِي عِنْدَكَ بَيْتًا فِي الْجَنَّةِ

رَبّ ابْنِ لِي عِنْدَكَ بَيْتًا فِي الْجَنَّةِ

Rabbi bni lī ʿindaka baytan fil jannah

My Lord! Build me a house in paradise near You.

[At-Tahrim 66:11]

When should you say this prayer?

⤷ When seeking a home in paradise, supplicating for eternal bliss in the afterlife, and expressing a desire for closeness to Allah.

رَبّ

Rabbi

رَبّ اغْفِرْ لِي وَلِوَالِدَيَّ وَلِلْمُؤْمِنِينَ

رَبِّ اغْفِرْ لِي وَلِوَالِدَيَّ وَلِلْمُؤْمِنِينَ

Rabbi ghfir lī wa liwālidayya wa lilmu'minīna

My Lord! Forgive me, my parents and all believers.

[Ibrahim 14:41]

When should you say this prayer?

When seeking forgiveness for oneself, parents, and all believers, expressing a collective plea for mercy and pardon.

رَبّ

Rabbi

رَبّ لَا تَذَرْنِي فَرْدًا وَأَنْتَ خَيْرُ الْوَارِثِينَ

رَبّ لَا تَذَرْنِي فَرْدًا وَأَنْتَ خَيْرُ الْوَارِثِينَ

Rabbi lā taðharnī farðan wa 'anta khayrul wārithīn

My Lord, do not leave me childless, though You are the best of heirs.

[Al-'Anbiyā' 21:89]

When should you say this prayer?

When fearing isolation or abandonment, seeking continuity in divine support, and recognising Allah as the ultimate and best inheritor.

رَبّ

Rabbi

رَبّ نَجِّنِي مِنَ الْقَوْمِ الظَّالِمِينَ

رَبِّ نَجِّنِي مِنَ الْقَوْمِ الظَّالِمِينَ

Robbi najjinī minal qawmi ẓālimīna

My Lord! Deliver me from the wrongdoing people.

[Al-Qasas 28:21]

When should you say this prayer?

When facing oppression or injustice from a group of people, seeking Allah's deliverance from the wrongdoing of the oppressors.

رَبّ

Rabbi

رَبِّ نَجِّنِي وَأَهْلِي مِمَّا يَعْمَلُونَ

رَبِّ نَجِّنِي وَأَهْلِي مِمَّا يَعْمَلُونَ

Rabbi najjinī wa 'ahlī mimmā yaʿ malūna

Lord, save me and my family from what they are doing.

[Ash-Shu'ara 26:169]

When should you say this prayer?

When seeking protection for oneself and family from the harmful actions of others, imploring Allah's safeguarding from external harm.

رَبّ

Rabbi

رَبِّ اجْعَلْنِي مُقِيمَ الصَّلَاةِ وَمِنْ ذُرِّيَّتِي رَبَّنَا وَتَقَبَّلْ دُعَاءِ

رَبِّ اجْعَلْنِي مُقِيمَ الصَّلَاةِ وَمِنْ ذُرِّيَّتِي رَبَّنَا وَتَقَبَّلْ دُعَاءِ

Rabbi j'alnī muqīmaṣ-ṣalāti wa min ðhurriyyatī rabbanā wa taqabbal du'ā'i

My Lord! Make me and those 'believers' of my descendants keep up prayer. Our Lord! Accept my prayers.

[Ibrahim 14:40]

When should you say this prayer?

When pleading for steadfastness in prayer and righteousness, and asking for acceptance of one's supplication for oneself and future generations.

رَبّ

Rabbi

رَبِّ بِمَا أَنْعَمْتَ عَلَيَّ فَلَنْ أَكُونَ ظَهِيرًا لِلْمُجْرِمِينَ

رَبِّ بِمَا أَنْعَمْتَ عَلَيَّ فَلَنْ أَكُونَ ظَهِيرًا لِلْمُجْرِمِينَ

*Rabbi bimā anʿ amta ʿalayya falan 'akūna
ẓahiran lil-mujrimina*

My Lord! For all Your favours upon me, I will never side with the wicked.

[Al-Qasas 28:17]

When should you say this prayer?

When gratefully acknowledging Allah's blessings, pledging not to support the wrongdoers, and expressing loyalty to divine principles.

رَبّ

Rabbi

رَبِّ هَبْ لي مِنْ لَدُنْكَ ذُرِّيَّةً طَيِّبَةً إنَّكَ سَميعُ الدُّعاءِ

رَبِّ هَبْ لي مِنْ لَدُنْكَ ذُرِّيَّةً طَيِّبَةً إنَّكَ سَميعُ الدُّعاءِ

Rabbi hab li min ladunka dhurriyyatan ṭayyibatan 'innaka samī'ud-du'a'i

My Lord! Grant me - by your grace - righteous offspring You are certainly the Hearer of all prayers.

[Ali 'Imran 3:38]

When should you say this prayer?

When requesting a righteous and virtuous offspring from Allah, acknowledging His ability to respond to supplications, and seeking a blessed lineage.

رَبّ

Rabbi

رَبِّ انْصُرْنِي عَلَى الْقَوْمِ الْمُفْسِدِينَ

رَبِّ انْصُرْنِي عَلَى الْقَوْمِ الْمُفْسِدِينَ

Rabbi nṣurnī ʿalāl-qawmil mufsidīna

My Lord! Help me against the people of corruption.

[Al-ʿAnkabut 29:30]

When should you say this prayer?

When facing a group of corrupt individuals or wrongdoers, seeking divine assistance and support in opposing those who spread mischief.

رَبّ

Rabbi

سُبْحَانَ رَبِّ السَّمَاوَاتِ وَٱلْأَرْضِ رَبِّ ٱلْعَرْشِ عَمَّا يَصِفُونَ

سُبْحَانَ رَبِّ السَّمَاوَاتِ وَالْأَرْضِ رَبِّ ٱلْعَرْشِ عَمَّا يَصِفُونَ

Subḥāna rabbi ssamāwāti wal-'arḍi rabbil lʿ arshi ʿammā yaṣifūna

Glorified is the Lord of the heavens and the earth, the Lord of the Throne, far above what they claim.

[Az-Zukhruf 43:82]

When should you say this prayer?

When expressing the perfection of Allah, recognising His transcendence over the heavens and the earth, and affirming His lordship over the mighty Throne.

رَبِّ

Rabbi

رَبِّ إِنِّي أَعُوذُ بِكَ
أَنْ أَسْأَلَكَ
مَا لَيْسَ لِي بِهِ عِلْمٌ
وَإِلَّا تَغْفِرْ لِي
وَتَرْحَمْنِي أَكُنْ مِنَ الْخَاسِرِينَ

رَبِّ إِنِّي أَعُوذُ بِكَ أَنْ أَسْأَلَكَ مَا لَيْسَ لِي بِهِ عِلْمٌ وَإِلَّا
تَغْفِرْ لِي وَتَرْحَمْنِي أَكُنْ مِنَ الْخَاسِرِينَ

Rabbi ʿinnī aʿūdhu bika ʿan ʿasʾalaka mā laysa lī bihi ʿilmun wa ʾillā taghfir lī wa tarḥamni ʾakun minal khāsirīna

Noah pleaded, "My Lord, I seek refuge in You from asking You about what I have no knowledge of, and unless You forgive me and have mercy on me, I will be one of the losers."

[Hud 11:47]

When should you say this prayer?

When faced with a decision or situation where one lacks knowledge, seeking refuge in Allah and asking for forgiveness to avoid making uninformed choices.

رَبّ

Rabbi

رَبِّ اغْفِرْ لِي
وَلِوَالِدَيَّ
وَلِمَنْ دَخَلَ بَيْتِي مُؤْمِنًا
وَلِلْمُؤْمِنِينَ وَالْمُؤْمِنَاتِ
وَلَا تَزِدِ الظَّالِمِينَ إِلَّا تَبَارًا

رَبِّ اغْفِرْ لِي وَلِوَالِدَيَّ وَلِمَنْ دَخَلَ بَيْتِي مُؤْمِنًا
وَلِلْمُؤْمِنِينَ وَالْمُؤْمِنَاتِ وَلَا تَزِدِ الظَّالِمِينَ إِلَّا تَبَارًا

Rabbi ghfir lī wa liwālidayya wa liman dakhala baytiya
muʾminan wa lilmuʾminīna wa lmuʾmināti walā tazididh-
dhālimīna ʾillā tabāran

Lord, forgive me, my parents, and whoever enters my house as a believer Forgive believing men and women but bring nothing but ruin down on the evildoers.

[Nuh 71:28]

When should you say this prayer?

Seeking forgiveness for oneself, parents, believers, and believers of both genders, while praying for mercy and not allowing oppressors to increase in wrongdoing.

رَبّ

Rabbi

رَبّ أَعُوذُ بِكَ مِنْ هَمَزَاتِ الشَّيَاطِينِ وَأَعُوذُ بِكَ رَبّ أَنْ يَحْضُرُونِ

رَبّ أَعُوذُ بِكَ مِنْ هَمَزَاتِ الشَّيَاطِينِ وَأَعُوذُ بِكَ رَبّ أَنْ يَحْضُرُونِ

*Rabbi 'aʿ ūdhu bika min hamazātish-shayāṭīni wa 'a
ʿudhu bika rabbi 'an yaḥḍurūni*

And I seek refuge in You, my Lord, that they even come near me.

[Al-Mu'minun 23:98]

When should you say this prayer?

When seeking protection from the whispers of evil forces and asking Allah to prevent them from approaching.

رَبّ

Rabbi

رَبِّ إِنِّي لَا أَمْلِكُ إِلَّا نَفْسِي وَأَخِي فَافْرُقْ بَيْنَنَا وَبَيْنَ الْقَوْمِ الْفَاسِقِينَ

رَبِّ إِنِّي لَا أَمْلِكُ إِلَّا نَفْسِي وَأَخِي فَافْرُقْ بَيْنَنَا وَبَيْنَ الْقَوْمِ الْفَاسِقِينَ

*Rabbi 'innī lā 'amliku 'illā nafsī wa 'akhī fafruq
baynanā wa baynal qawmil fāsiqīna*

**Moses pleaded, "My Lord! I have
no control over anyone except
myself and my brother. So set us
apart from the rebellious people."**

[Al-Ma'idah 5:25]

When should you say this prayer?

When facing a situation of potential
conflict or division among oneself and
others who engage in sinful
behaviour.

رَبّ

Rabbi

رَبِّ اجْعَلْ هَذَا بَلَدًا آمِنًا وَارْزُقْ أَهْلَهُ مِنَ الثَّمَرَاتِ مَنْ آمَنَ مِنْهُمْ بِاللَّهِ وَالْيَوْمِ الْآخِرِ

رَبِّ اجْعَلْ هَذَا بَلَدًا آمِنًا وَارْزُقْ أَهْلَهُ مِنَ الثَّمَرَاتِ مَنْ آمَنَ مِنْهُمْ بِاللَّهِ وَالْيَوْمِ الْآخِرِ

Rabbi j ʿal hādhā baladan ʾāminan warzuq ʾahlahu minath-thamarāti man ʾāmana minhum billāhi wal-yawmil ʾākhiri

"My Lord, make this city (of Mecca) secure and provide fruits to its people — those among them who believe in Allah and the Last Day.

[Al-Baqarah 2:126]

When should you say this prayer?

When praying for the safety and prosperity of a city or community, asking Allah to make it secure and provide sustenance for those who believe in Him and the Last Day.

رَبِّ

Rabbi

رَبِّ احْكُمْ بِالْحَقِّ وَرَبُّنَا الرَّحْمَانُ الْمُسْتَعَانُ عَلَى مَا تَصِفُونَ

بِالْحَقِّ وَرَبُّنَا الرَّحْمَانُ الْمُسْتَعَانُ عَلَى مَا رَبِّ احْكُمْ تَصِفُونَ

*Rabbi ḥkum bil-ḥaqqi wa rabbunār-raḥmānul
musta ʿānu ʾalā mā taṣifūna*

"My Lord! Judge (between us) in truth. And our Lord is the Most Compassionate, Whose help is sought against what you claim."

[Al-Anbya 21:112]

When should you say this prayer?

When seeking Allah's judgment based on truth and relying on His mercy to assist against false accusations or claims.

رَبّ

Rabbi

رَبِّ اغْفِرْ لِي وَلِأَخِي وَأَدْخِلْنَا فِي رَحْمَتِكَ وَأَنْتَ أَرْحَمُ الرَّاحِمِينَ

رَبِّ اغْفِرْ لِي وَلِأَخِي وَأَدْخِلْنَا فِي رَحْمَتِكَ وَأَنْتَ أَرْحَمُ الرَّاحِمِينَ

*Rabbi ghfir lī wa li 'akhī wa 'aɗkhilnā fī raḥmatika
wa 'anta 'arḥamur-rāḥimīna*

My Lord! Forgive me and my brother! And admit us into Your mercy You are the Most Merciful of the merciful.

[Al-Aʿrāf 7:151]

When should you say this prayer?

When seeking forgiveness and mercy for oneself and one's brother, asking to be admitted into Allah's mercy, the most merciful.

رَبّ

Rabbi

رَبِّ اغْفِرْ لِي وَهَبْ لِي مُلْكًا لَا يَنْبَغِي لِأَحَدٍ مِنْ بَعْدِي إِنَّكَ أَنْتَ الْوَهَّابُ

رَبِّ اغْفِرْ لِي وَهَبْ لِي مُلْكًا لَا يَنْبَغِي لِأَحَدٍ مِنْ بَعْدِي إِنَّكَ أَنْتَ الْوَهَّابُ

*Rabbi ghfir lī wahab lī mulkan lā yanbaghī li 'ahadin
min ba' dī 'innaka 'antal-wahhābu*

**Lord forgive me! Grant me such
power as no one after me will have
- You are the Most Generous
Provider.**

[Sād 38:35]

When should you say this prayer?

> When seeking forgiveness and asking
Allah to grant a kingdom that is not
fit for anyone else after oneself.

رَبّ

Rabbi

رَبّ إِنَّ ابْنِي مِنْ أَهْلِي
وَإِنَّ وَعْدَكَ الْحَقُّ
وَأَنْتَ أَحْكَمُ الْحَاكِمِينَ

رَبّ إِنَّ ابْنِي مِنْ أَهْلِي وَإِنَّ وَعْدَكَ الْحَقُّ وَأَنْتَ
أَحْكَمُ الْحَاكِمِينَ

*Rabbi 'inna bnī min 'ahlī wa 'inna wa ʿ∂akal-ḥaqqu
wa 'anta aḥkamul ḥākimīna*

"My Lord! Certainly my son is (also) of my family, Your promise is surely true, and You are the most just of all judges!"

[Hud 11:45]

When should you say this prayer?

When entrusting a loved one, especially a child, to Allah's care. It echoes Prophet Ibrahim's trust in Allah's true promise and ultimate wisdom when leaving his family in a barren valley. It expresses confidence in Allah as the Best of Judges in situations requiring divine guidance.

رَبّ

Rabbi

رَبِّ إِنَّهُنَّ أَضْلَلْنَ كَثِيرًا مِنَ النَّاسِ فَمَنْ تَبِعَنِي فَإِنَّهُ مِنِّي وَمَنْ عَصَانِي فَإِنَّكَ غَفُورٌ رَّحِيمٌ

رَبِّ إِنَّهُنَّ أَضْلَلْنَ كَثِيرًا مِنَ النَّاسِ فَمَنْ تَبِعَنِي فَإِنَّهُ مِنِّي وَمَنْ عَصَانِي فَإِنَّكَ غَفُورٌ رَّحِيمٌ

Rabbi 'innahunna 'aḍlalna kathīran minan-nāsi faman tabi ʿanī fa 'innahu minnī wa man ʿaṣānī fa'inaka ghafūrun raḥīmun

My Lord! They have caused many people to go astray. So whoever follows me is with me, and whoever disobeys me —then surely You are (still) All-Forgiving, Most Merciful.

[Ibrahim 14:36]

When should you say this prayer?

This prayer is attributed to Prophet Nuh (Noah) in the context of his plea to Allah. Facing the challenge of guiding people who had gone astray, Prophet Nuh seeks Allah's mercy and forgiveness. He asks for blessings on those who follow him and acknowledges Allah's forgiving and merciful nature for those who disobey.

رَبّ

Rabbi

رَبِّ أَدْخِلْنِي مُدْخَلَ صِدْقٍ وَأَخْرِجْنِي مُخْرَجَ صِدْقٍ وَاجْعَلْ لِي مِن لَدُنْكَ سُلْطَانًا نَصِيرًا

رَبِّ أَدْخِلْنِي مُدْخَلَ صِدْقٍ وَأَخْرِجْنِي مُخْرَجَ صِدْقٍ
وَاجْعَلْ لِي مِنْ لَدُنْكَ سُلْطَانًا نَصِيرًا

*Rabbi 'adkhilnī mudkhala ṣidqin wa 'akhrijnī mukhraja
ṣidqin waj'al-lī min ladunka ṣultānan naṣīran*

And say, "My Lord! Grant me an honourable entrance and an honourable exit1 and give me a supporting authority from Yourself."

[Al-Isra 17:80]

When should you say this prayer?

Seeking entry into situations of truth and exit from situations of falsehood, asking Allah to provide support and authority.

رَبّ

Rabbi

رَبِّ أَوْزِعْنِي أَنْ أَشْكُرَ
نِعْمَتَكَ الَّتِي أَنْعَمْتَ عَلَيَّ
وَعَلَى وَالِدَيَّ وَأَنْ أَعْمَلَ
صَالِحًا تَرْضَاهُ وَأَدْخِلْنِي بِرَحْمَتِكَ
فِي عِبَادِكَ الصَّالِحِينَ

رَبِّ أَوْزِعْنِي أَنْ أَشْكُرَ نِعْمَتَكَ الَّتِي أَنْعَمْتَ عَلَيَّ وَعَلَى وَالِدَيَّ وَأَنْ أَعْمَلَ صَالِحًا تَرْضَاهُ وَأَدْخِلْنِي بِرَحْمَتِكَ فِي عِبَادِكَ الصَّالِحِينَ

*Rabbi 'awzi'nī 'an 'ashkura ni'matakal-latī 'an'amta
'alayya wa 'alā wālidayya wa 'an a'mala ṣāliḥan tardāhu
wa 'adkhilnī biraḥmatika fī 'ibādikaṣ-ṣāliḥīna*

**O Lord, inspire me to be thankful
for the blessings You have granted
me and my parents, and to do good
deeds that please You; admit me by
Your grace into the ranks of Your
righteous servants.**

[An-Naml 27:19]

When should you say this prayer?

When seeking guidance to be grateful for
Allah's blessings and to perform
righteous deeds that please Him, while
asking for inclusion among the righteous.

رَبّ

Rabbi

رَبِّ قَدْ آتَيْتَنِي مِنَ الْمُلْكِ
وَعَلَّمْتَنِي مِن تَأْوِيلِ الْأَحَادِيثِ
فَاطِرَ السَّمَاوَاتِ وَالْأَرْضِ
أَنتَ وَلِيِّي فِي الدُّنْيَا وَالْآخِرَةِ
تَوَفَّنِي مُسْلِمًا وَأَلْحِقْنِي
بِالصَّالِحِينَ

رَبِّ قَدْ آتَيْتَنِي مِنَ الْمُلْكِ وَعَلَّمْتَنِي مِن تَأْوِيلِ
الْأَحَادِيثِ ۚ فَاطِرَ السَّمَاوَاتِ وَالْأَرْضِ أَنتَ وَلِيِّي فِي
الدُّنْيَا وَالْآخِرَةِ ۖ تَوَفَّنِي مُسْلِمًا وَأَلْحِقْنِي بِالصَّالِحِينَ

*Rabbi qaд 'ātaytani minal mulki wa ʿallamtani min ta
'wīlil 'aḥādīthi. Fāṭiras-samāwāti wal 'arдi 'anta
waliyyī fiд-дunyā wal-'akhirati. tawaffanī musliman
wa 'alḥiqni bissālihīna*

My Lord! You have surely granted me authority and taught me the interpretation of dreams.

[Yusuf 12:101]

When should you say this prayer?

When acknowledging Allah as the Bestower of dominion and knowledge, seeking guidance, and asking for death in a state of submission to Allah, joined with the righteous.

رَبِّ

Rabbi

رَبِّ هَبْ لِي حُكْمًا وَأَلْحِقْنِي بِالصَّالِحِينَ

رَبِّ هَبْ لِي حُكْمًا وَأَلْحِقْنِي بِالصَّالِحِينَ

وَاجْعَلْ لِي لِسَانَ صِدْقٍ فِي الْآخِرِينَ وَاجْعَلْنِي مِنْ وَرَثَةِ جَنَّةِ النَّعِيمِ

وَاجْعَلْ لِي لِسَانَ صِدْقٍ فِي الْآخِرِينَ وَاجْعَلْنِي مِنْ وَرَثَةِ جَنَّةِ النَّعِيمِ

Rabbi hab lī ḥukman wa 'alḥiqnī biṣṣāliḥīna waj 'allī lisāna ṣidqin fil 'ākhirina wa j'alni min warathati jannatin-naī̄ īmi

My Lord! Grant me wisdom, and join me with the righteous. Bless me with honourable mention among later generations.

[Ash-Shu'ara 26:83-84]

When should you say this prayer?

When seeking wisdom and righteous companionship, asking to be joined with the virtuous and granted the ability to speak the truth among people.

About the Author

Mourad Diouri is an author and teaching fellow of Arabic at the University of Edinburgh in Scotland, UK. In addition to writing instructional books on learning Arabic as a foreign language, he also works as an education consultant, external examiner and teacher trainer within the UK and internationally. He lives in Edinburgh, Scotland, with his wife and children.

Also by Mourad Diouri

An ABC of Quotes About Palestine: Exploring Voices on Palestine & the Palestinian Quest for Justice (2023)

My First Arabic Numbers Reader & Colouring Book, (2023)

An Abc of Palestine: A Journey To Discover Palestine & The Palestinian People For Kids & Grown Ups (2023)

My First Arabic Colours: Reader & Activity Book for Kids, (2023)

My Journey Through The Most Beautiful Names of Allah: Arabic Reader & Activity Book for Kids: **(Volume 1, 2 & 3)** (2023)

My Arabic Learning Journals: My Abc Dictionary (English-Arabic), (2022)

My First Arabic Alphabet & Colouring Book [Arabic for Little Ones] (2023)

My Arabic Learning Journals: My Abc Dictionary (Arabic-English), (2022)

My Arabic Animal Alphabet Reader, Arabic for Little Ones, (2023)

My Arabic Learning Journals: Thematic Vocabulary, (2022)

My First Arabic Alphabet Reader, Arabic for Little Ones, (2023)

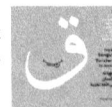

Tricky Tongue Twisters In Arabic (Arabic Script & Sounds),[Essential Arabic Readers] (2023)

My First Arabic Alphabet: Letter Tracing & Colouring Book [Arabic for Little Ones] (2023)

I Am .... An ABC of Empowering Self-Affirmations: A Guided Journal for Self-Discovery, Self-Growth & Resilience (2022)

Essential Arabic Readers: Alphabet Letters with Vowels & Pronunciation Symbols, (2022)

My Journey through Ramadan & Eid Al-Fitr (Arabic for Little Ones), Mosaic Tree Press (2023)

Similar Sounding Letters in Arabic: Essential Arabic Readers (2023)

CoronaVirus Lexicon: A Practical Guide for Arabic Learners & Translators (M. Diouri & M. Aboelezz 2023)

Essential Arabic Readers: Arabic Alphabet Writing Practice Handbook, (2023)

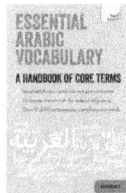

Teach Yourself: Essential Arabic Vocabulary: A Handbook of Core Terms, Hodder Education (2015)

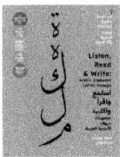

Listen, Read & Write: Arabic Alphabet Letter Groups [Essential Arabic Readers] (2023)

Internet Arabic: Essential Middle Eastern Vocabularies (w/ MP3 CD), Edinburgh University Press (2013)

Arabic & Islamic Mosaic & Calligraphy Colouring Journal (Volume 1: Islamic Quotes) (2022)

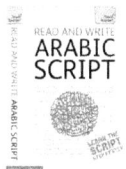

Teach Yourself: Read & Write Arabic Script, Hodder Education (2011)

Browse our full catalogue at

MosaicTree.org

A | Arabic Script & Sounds

A-Z | Arabic Vocabulary

Arabic for Little Ones

Arabic/Islamic Mosaic & Calligraphy

Arabic Learning Journals

Well-Being & Character Development

Mosaic Tree Press
MosaicTree.org

بحمد الله تم

Completed with the grace of God

www.ingramcontent.com/pod-product-compliance
Lightning Source LLC
LaVergne TN
LVHW051755080426
835511LV00018B/3328